PRAYERS

of

Faith

Contributing Writers

Nancy Parker Brummett

Lain Ehmann

Marie D. Jones

Publications International, Ltd.

Cover Photo: Artville

Contributing Writers

Nancy Parker Brummett is a freelance writer, columnist, and the author of four books who lives in Colorado Springs, CO. Leading women closer to the heart of God is the hallmark of her speaking and writing ministries. To learn more about her life and work, visit www.nancyparkerbrummett.com.

Lain Ehmann is a Massachusetts-based writer and mom to three.

Marie D. Jones is the author of several best-selling nonfiction books, and a contributing author to numerous inspirational books, including *Echoes of Love: Sisters, Mother, Grandmother, Friends, Graduation, Wedding; Mother's Daily Prayer Book;* and *When You Lose Someone You Love: God Will Comfort You.* She can be reached at www.mariedjones.com.

Acknowledgments

FAITH IS BELIEVING THAT GOD WILL NEVER FAIL US

Faith is believing in what one cannot see. Faith in God is trusting him even when our perceptions are contrary to his promises. When our heads tell us something cannot be done, faith sees us through to achieve our goal. When we think there will be no end to our suffering, faith pushes us forward and through the pain to the other side.

Meanwhile, God's faith in us never ceases; indeed, he believes in each one of us. This is good news, for when our own faith wavers, and we all go through times when it does, we can turn to God for that extra faith we need to make it through. Knowing that God is on our side, the impossible becomes possible and the insurmountable can be overcome.

Faith is more priceless than all material things, for faith can move mountains and calm stormy seas. When we put our belief in God, he empowers us to face any challenge and come out victorious in the end.

Though we cannot see it, faith is always there, acting as a rock that anchors and grounds us in the certainty that we cannot fail with God on our side. Faith is our constant and ever-present cheerleader, a force that says "yes" when the rest of the world tells us "no."

Faith is believing that God is with us, gently and lovingly reminding us that if we let him take the wheel, we will never be alone on the road of life.

Dear God, it's hard to keep the faith when I see everything around me falling apart. I know that faith is belief in things unseen, but I find it difficult to hold on to the unseen when what I see is causing me so much trouble. Help me find the courage to get through this. I have faith in you and want to have faith in myself to meet any challenges I encounter. Please, if I get weak, let me lean on you for a while until I am strong enough again to rise up and do what needs to be done. I think that together we can do anything, God. I put my faith in you. Amen.

O Lord, how often I turn to you when I don't know where else to turn! If only I would always turn to you first. My faith in you is a constant in my life, and yet too often I let other influences distract me and lead me away from a total reliance on you. I know in my heart that it is in you, and you only, that I'm protected and safe. Please shelter me, Lord! You are the only

place I want to run to in times of trouble. My
faith rests entirely in you.

⇒ ⇐

*You are a hiding place for me; you preserve me
from trouble; you surround me with
glad cries of deliverance.*
—Psalm 32:7

⇒ ⇐

Dear God, despite my best efforts and inten-
tions, sometimes my path strays from yours.
I fall into sin, and I'm ashamed of my weak-
ness. But I come to you in faith and repentance,
trusting that you will dust me off and open
your arms wide, welcoming me back into your
fold. I don't need to fear making mistakes, for
you are a merciful and loving God, who longs
to help me in my journey toward Christ. Thank
you for your continued love for me and for
making me one of your children.

I have faith in you, Lord Jesus, for you have never let me down. My faith makes me strong and fills me with the courage and fortitude I need to get through life's more pressing problems. Your faith in me is like a beacon that I move toward, helping my eyes focus on the prize of your love and on your assistance in all that I do. Knowing that I'm not alone helps me be a pillar of strength for others as well, as they discover their own lost faith in you. I have faith in you, Lord. You always come through for me. Thank you.

Then your light shall break forth like the dawn, and your healing shall spring up quickly; your vindicator shall go before you, the glory of the Lord shall be your rear guard.
—Isaiah 58:8

Lord, again today I had a conversation with someone who seems to be putting her faith into all the wrong things. Yes, her life may be improved temporarily by a different diet or another exercise program, but if those things are all she has, Lord, she is missing out on so much more. She may even find inspiration in some of the self-help books she buys, but in the end, she can't find meaning in herself alone. Thank you, Lord, that you make yourself available to all who are willing to put their faith in you. Please reach my friend, and give her the courage to believe in you.

Dear Lord, whenever I face challenges to my faith, I wonder why you would allow me to be tested. I've already committed my life to you—isn't that enough? But then I realize that a faith untested is no faith at all and that it is

necessary for me to go through difficult times
in order to strengthen my resolve and my com-
mitment to the Christian life. So now, I welcome these times. I know they will be tough,
but I also know that with your help I will prevail over every temptation. Thank you for giving me these opportunities to grow in faith and
to learn to rely on you more and more. Amen.

*For the Lord will not reject for ever. Although he
causes grief, he will have compassion according
to the abundance of his steadfast love.*
—Lamentations 3:31–32

When other people let me down, Father in
Heaven, it is good to know that I can always
count on you to get me by. Sometimes my
friends and family are too busy or distracted
to deal with my simple needs, so in prayer

I come to you asking for your understanding and for an increased faith in your devotion to me. There are too few people and things in life we can depend on, but I believe you will always be there for me when I need it. Thank you, loving Father, for giving me something truly wonderful to believe in.

Dear God, sometimes I wonder if you just shake your head when you see our meager attempts to help others. So often we are giving them just what they need to survive the day, but holding back in terms of offering them the abundance that can be theirs through faith in you. When we reach out to others in love, God, let us also reach out with faith and be willing to share the faith that sustains us. Then and only then will all their needs be met. In your Son's most precious name I pray. Amen.

*The only thing that counts is faith
working through love.*
—Galatians 5:6

Dear Lord, I have been fighting these battles
for so long, and now I can see the glimmer
of change on the horizon. My faith has been
rewarded and my energy is renewed because
your kingdom on earth is closer than ever. I
trust that everything is unfolding moment by
moment according to your holy plan. I just
need to stay the course until your time is at
hand. Thank you, Father, for your goodness.

My Lord, please strengthen my faith so that
nothing will disturb the calm waters in my
heart. Make me a rock that does not move no
matter how hard the waves crash up against it.
During stormy days in my life, strengthen my

faith so I will refuse to give up. Build my faith into a foundation that cannot be shaken so that I can be a rock to someone else today. Amen.

The time is surely coming, says the Lord, when the one who plows shall overtake the one who reaps, and the treader of grapes the one who sows the seed; the mountains shall drip sweet wine, and all the hills shall flow with it.
—Amos 9:13

Dear Father in Heaven, how often our faith seems utterly depleted! We come to you asking for more faith, but we ask for such a small amount. You are willing to douse us in life-giving faith, but we come asking for just what we can carry in our cupped hands. We ask for a bit of faith for a certain situation or the faith to get us through the next task at hand. Immerse us in a complete renewal of our faith, Lord! Let our faith in you empower us—heart, mind, and soul—that others may see you in all we do.

Heavenly Father, I sometimes fear that the darkness is overcoming the light in our world and that all good things will be extinguished. At times like these, I need only to return to you, refreshing my faith in your holy Word. You are all-powerful, and righteousness will prevail. I trust in you, my Lord, and I know that I'm on the side of the Prince of Peace, who brings me comfort.

They are not afraid of evil tidings;
their hearts are firm, secure in the Lord.
Their hearts are steady, they will not be afraid;
in the end they will look in triumph on their foes.
—Psalm 112:7–8

So many times in my life, Lord, I have felt my faith drain out of me, leaving me feeling high and dry. Lost and afraid, I have wandered alone and felt the abandonment of those I thought were my friends. I pray that you will never abandon me and that you will strengthen my faith again so that I will never feel horribly alone. I know that you are always with me, but my heart and my soul need to be reminded of that daily, especially when things get chaotic and I feel as if I am at the end of my rope. Give me the faith I need to get through one day at a time, for I know that will be enough.

My Heavenly Father, there are few aspects of our lives that are constant. The political scene shifts with each election. Careers seem to be heading in a positive direction and then abruptly end. Fortunes rise and fall. Even relationships sometimes reach their peaks and then fade away. But you, O Lord, never change! Your power and your majesty always were and always will be. Thank you, Lord, that when we put our faith in you, we are never disappointed.

⊱ ⊰

From everlasting to everlasting you are God.
—Psalm 90:2

⊱ ⊰

Lord Jesus, I often wonder how, with our limited capacity for understanding and our earthly weaknesses, we can ever accomplish all the work necessary in preparation for your return. Then I remember what you told us: that even the smallest bit of faith is magnified and made powerful in you. We do not need to worry about how things will be accomplished; we need only to show up with our hands out-stretched, ready to put our trust in you. I may not think I can move mountains, but with your power, I can do anything. Please use me for your purposes today and every day.

God, I feel terribly lost. I'm stuck in this dark place of sadness and hopelessness, and my faith is nowhere to be found. I ask in prayer for your loving assistance—that you may return to me the faith that can move mountains and overcome any obstacle. I have many obstacles to overcome, and I have no idea how to do it. Please help me find that faith that reminds me that I'm never alone, that you can get me through this, and that I will be the better for it.

I will plant them upon their land, and they shall never again be plucked up out of the land that I have given them.
—Amos 9:15

Thank you, God, for showing me once again that when I place my faith entirely in others I will only be disappointed. Even the most wonderful spouse anyone could ask for will eventually do something thoughtless. The politicians and celebrities we admire fall hard when they stumble, mostly because we have put them on such unrealistic pedestals and put so much faith in them. Thank you for the reminder that while it enriches our lives to admire or love others, it is you who should be the center of our faith. In Jesus' name, I pray. Amen.

Dear Lord, when I need you, I call your name and you are with me. You will never leave my side. You know my every desire and want before I know them myself. My faith in you is steadfast. As long as I continue to trust in you, my future is secure and no bad thing can overcome me. I ask that you watch over me as you have always done, all the days of my life.

⤙ ⤚

The Lord is near to all who call on him,
to all who call on him in truth.
He fulfills the desire of all who fear him;
he also hears their cry, and saves them.
—Psalm 145:18–19

⤙ ⤚

I wear my faith draped over me like a powerful robe, dear God in Heaven, that can make mountains move out of my way and part the waters before me. My faith keeps me strong and purposeful, always bringing me through the dark valleys into the sunlight again. My faith in you, loving God, is my mighty power, which I use for only the highest and the best good. I pray that my faith in you might be a beacon for others to follow, should they ever lose their own faith, to remind them that, like me, they are never without your presence or your love. Amen.

⟶ ⟵

My Lord, what a joy it was to be able to visit the Holy Land and walk in places you are said to have walked! How inspiring to gaze out on the Sea of Galilee where you calmed the storm and to see the hillside where thousands gathered around to hear you teach the beatitudes! We never saw you, Lord, but we saw where you lived. Yet as meaningful as that experience was, we believed even before we journeyed there, for we see you everywhere in the faces of all those who believe in you and put their faith in you. Thank you, Lord, that we don't have to travel to the Holy Land to believe. We just have to open the doors to our hearts and welcome you in.

⟶ ⟵

Blessed are those who have not seen and yet
have come to believe.
—John 20:29

Heavenly Father, I have discovered that when my faith seems in short supply, I can still trust you, and then my faith actually grows. When I find myself falling into the pattern of ruminating and obsessing over the details of how a particular circumstance will work out, I remind myself to turn to you, and suddenly I find my faith becomes strong again. Thank you for these little ways in which you strengthen my relationship with you. With all my heart, I love you.

Dear Lord, my faith is hard to come by these days. I struggle to hold on to the little faith I have when times become as trying as they have been lately. That is why I turn to you today in prayer, because in the past you have always restored my lost faith when I wavered and weakened during the trials I was facing. I know that when I call upon you, my prayers will always be answered and a strong and fresh dose of faith will be delivered to me right away. For this I am grateful, Lord. Amen.

Jesus answered them, "Truly I tell you, if you have faith and do not doubt, not only will you do what has been done to the fig tree, but even if you say to this mountain, 'Be lifted up and thrown into the sea,' it will be done."
—Matthew 21:21

Dear Lord God, when we look at your faithfulness we truly stand in awe. No matter how seriously we take the promises we make or how

dedicated we are to those we love, our faithfulness is pitiful and paltry compared to yours.
You, O Lord, are truly faithful! You are faithful to forgive. You are faithful to fulfill all your
promises to your people. And you will be faithful to the end of the world. Thank you, Lord,
for your faithfulness to all generations, now and
forever. Amen.

Supreme Lord of the universe, today I stand
strong and proclaim your glory. My faith in you
makes me strong, and I can't help but share my
trust and love for you with others. You are the
sovereign Lord, and all that you declare shall
come to pass. Nothing can withstand your will,
and I'm thankful to align myself with you. I'm
in awe of your power and glory, and my heart
is full of your Holy Spirit. When I read your
Word, I'm reassured of your promises to me.
I want nothing more than to live as a follower
of Christ until the end of my days.

*God did not give us a spirit of cowardice, but
rather a spirit of power and of love
and of self-discipline.*
—2 Timothy 1:7

Heavenly Father, I put my faith in you, for you
are my rock and my foundation. I know that
upon you I can always stand firm, even as the
ground surrounding me shakes and trembles.
I will not fall, for your arms embrace me faithfully, and I will not have to deal with my challenges alone. It is good to know I am always
cared for and that even when things look as
though they are falling apart, with my faith in
you, I will soon see that my life is really coming together. My faith in you makes me strong,
God. Thank you.

Father God, when will we learn that the greatest gift we can pass to our children and our grandchildren is not our earthly wealth but our faith in you? We set up trust funds and college funds, or we feel badly when we can't, when the only true security is through you! As parents and grandparents, keep us focused on what really matters. Remind us to spend precious time with the younger generation—to earn the right to share the greatest legacy we have to give, which is faith in you.

So even to old age and gray hairs, O God, do not forsake me, until I proclaim your might to all the generations to come.
—Psalm 71:18

Father, I have so little to offer you in return
for your greatest sacrifice, the gift of your Son,
Jesus Christ. I am nothing compared to the
power that resides in you, and yet you long to
have a relationship with me. Because of your
longing for me, I willingly give you the only
gift I have—the gift of myself. I lay my faith
at your feet in offering and supplication, and I
hope that it will be found worthy in your sight.
All that I am, all that I have, is due to you.

In joy I celebrate my steadfast faith in you,
Heavenly Father, and I know you have faith in
me. You have shown me your faith by trusting
me with so many lessons and challenges, and
I have done my best to be worthy of your faith.
I celebrate the knowledge that even when my
world seems to be chaotic and crazy, there is
an unseen force of peace and love I can always
depend on to help me get through. My faith is
my foundation. Thank you for the gift of faith.

*Come and see what God has done: he is awesome
in his deeds among mortals. He turned the sea into
dry land; they passed through the river on foot.*
—Psalm 66:5–6

Almighty God, how well I know that going
out in faith means we don't always know where
we are going or what will happen once we get
there. A life of faith may begin with a leap,
but it's lived out step by step as we trust in you
to show us where to go next. Your Word is a
light to my path, Lord. Fellowship with other
believers guides me, and so does the counsel of
the Holy Spirit when I turn to you in prayer.
Thank you, Lord God, that living a life of
faith is never boring but is always an incred-
ible adventure. And thank you for directing my
steps of faith.

Father in Heaven, if ever I feel far from you,
I just need to quiet my mind and heart and
wait for you to speak. You are always with me,
but sometimes your voice gets drowned out by
the busyness of my day. Your faithful presence
is constant, and if I look deeply enough, I will
find you. It is because of your very strength that
you do not force me to worship you; instead,
you wait for me to come to you. And when
I do, you are always there, just waiting to welcome me home. Let me return to you again
and again, every day.

Be still, and know that I am God!
I am exalted among the nations,
I am exalted in the earth.
—Psalm 46:10

To those who have faith, more good things shall be given. Faith in you, God, multiplies blessings and makes the old shine like new again. To those who have faith, nothing is impossible under the sun, and all things can be overcome. To those who have faith, love and hope are never far from sight, even when it seems they have abandoned us. To those who have faith in you, God, the kingdom is set out before us to live amidst the infinite abundance and unlimited prosperity of your promises. Thanks be to you, the one, true God.

O Lord, how my heart goes out to those who are in the midst of losing a loved one without the blessed assurance of eternal life! It can be terribly painful to watch someone we love fading away before our eyes. But because of faith in you, O Lord, we know this is not the only life we live. There is so much more to come—an eternity, in fact! Thank you, Lord, for the guarantee of eternal life. It's not only a blessing to us when we die, but it also allows us to grieve with hope when we lose those we love and who love you, for you are welcoming them into your heavenly kingdom.

We look not at what can be seen but at what cannot be seen; for what can be seen is temporary, but what cannot be seen is eternal.
—2 Corinthians 4:18

Sovereign Lord, my faith shines bright as a star today. I can feel it radiating from my very soul. Nothing can conquer me or shake my trust in you. By accepting your Son, Jesus Christ, as my Savior, I have already vanquished the biggest foe of all. Now I can rest in you, my protector and guardian, until the end of my days.

Just as children have faith in their parents to
love them and watch over them, I have faith in
you, Father God, to always love me, too. I look
up to you for wisdom and guidance, and I pray
to you for patience and understanding. You
always come through for me in wondrous ways,
proving to me that my faith is well placed. As
your beloved child, I feel nourished and protected by your love, and I will always believe in
you, just as you always believe in me. Amen.

*Truly I tell you, unless you change and become
like children, you will never enter the kingdom of
heaven. Whoever becomes humble like this child is
the greatest in the kingdom of heaven.*
—Matthew 18:3–4

Though the fig tree does not blossom, and no fruit is on the vines; though the produce of the olive fails, and the fields yield no food; though the flock is cut off from the fold, and there is no herd in the stalls, yet I will rejoice in the Lord; I will exult in the God of my salvation. God, the Lord, is my strength; he makes my feet like the feet of a deer, and makes me tread upon the heights.

—Habakkuk 3:17–19

O God, my spirit is shattered! I cannot even begin to put the millions of pieces back together. I am scared that everything I hold dear will be taken from me, and I will be left, loveless and broken. I turn to your Word for solace, and you tell me to keep steady in my faith. If I remain true to you, recovery will come, day by day, with your help. Please be with me in this dark period, giving me comfort and reassuring me of your presence. I ask in Jesus' precious name. Amen.

I am grateful to Christ Jesus our Lord, who has strengthened me, because he judged me faithful and appointed me to his service, even though I was formerly a blasphemer, a persecutor, and a man of violence. But I received mercy because I had acted ignorantly in unbelief, and the grace of our Lord overflowed for me with the faith and love that are in Christ Jesus. The saying is sure and worthy of full acceptance, that Christ Jesus came into the world to save sinners—of whom I am the foremost. But for that very reason I received mercy, so that in me, as the foremost, Jesus Christ might display utmost patience, making me an example to those who would come to believe in him for eternal life.
—1 Timothy 1:12–16

He heals the brokenhearted,
and binds up their wounds.
—Psalm 147:3

O Lord Jesus, thank you for all the monuments to faith you have strategically placed in my life. Whenever I feel myself beginning to doubt that you will intervene in a given situation, all I have to do is look back and remember when you were faithful in the past. Crises with teenagers, the pain of financial reverses, grieving the loss of friends and parents—I reflect on all those times and see how you faithfully worked to bring me safely through them and closer to you at the same time. Looking back increases my faith going forward, Lord. I praise you for the monuments of faith.